Bachelard Interpreted 2

A Cleansing Flame

Frank Prem

Wild Arancini Press
2024

Publication Details

Title: A Cleansing Flame: Bachelard Interpreted Book 2
ISBN: 978-1-923166-24-0 (p-bk)
ISBN: 978-1-925963-88-5 (e-bk)

Published by Wild Arancini Press
Copyright © 2024 Frank Prem
All rights reserved

Cover Concept: Wild Arancini Press
Cover Image AI assistant: Adobe Firefly

In the fire lies the light.

CONTENTS

A Cleansing Flame

The Flame of a Candle

The Psychoanalysis of Fire

Fragments from A Poetics of Fire

A Cleansing Flame

Introduction

French scientist and philosopher Gaston Bachelard (1884 - 1962) explored and examined poetics and poetry in great depth over the course of his lifetime, particularly examining the poetics of natural elements, of which he identified the four that are traditionally considered:

Fire
Water
Air
Earth

In addition, however, he (effectively) identified two further elements, or dimensions, for his examination:

Time
Space

The *Bachelard Interpreted* poetry series responds to each of these elements and dimensions, as well as encompassing some of Bachelard's further scientific and literary interests.

A Cleansing Flame explores the poetic nature of flame and fire in the context of reverie and contemplation. In this collection, we focus on the dance of flame, yellows, reds and blues and visit times before reliance on electricity and artificial luminescence to provide our lights and guides.

Be prepared to sleep, to dream, to transform into your other — fire-dreaming — self through A *Cleansing Flame*

Note: A *Cleansing Flame* is one of a series of poetry collections inspired by the work of Gaston Bachelard. References to the Bachelard translations that have been relied on as source materials for this project are listed at the end of this book.

The Flame of a Candle

renewal (by flame)

dulled in heart
listless . . .

he searched

haphazardly

dispiritedly

> *a drawer*
> *a bench top*
>
> *beneath loose papers*

a slow ordeal
ill-directed
and half —
almost —
abandoned mid-task

but his hands
arrived
finally
at the small box
with flint-lined sides
and a single remaining
wax-headed
match

his hand shook
a little
as he made the commitment
and struck

> *sulphur to flint*
>
> *sizzle to flare*

at the spread of the light —
its stability—
he too steadied

applied the burning stick
to his candle stub —
already almost devoured —

last match

last scratch and burn
but
for now —
gazing into the living
spirit —
he was renewed

forging a memento

with a hand outstretched
she approached
the warmth

more intense
as she moved nearer

watching
fully mesmerised

closer closer
from warm
to sear

the gyre
drew her
as a compulsion

she could not withdraw

the finger
so sensitive
extended

one touch

    so

a broken spell

it was only once
but *so* impassioned

the burn
some salutary news

but the fever
of the the movement —
just once —

just once

a memento
to re-touch
re-call
through all her life

lumpen

he is a lumpen man
clumsy in his doings
crude in the way he speaks . . .

the things he sees

labouring
over manual movements
machine operations
the mechanics

noise

whine and roar and yell
and bray
so loud
over the funniest thing
you ever saw or heard

      ho ho ho
      ha ha

he is
a lumpen man

dirt and dust and beer
and the wind
that must be passed

his overalls at home
cast to the floor
in a dirty corner
of the laundry room

and so
to the fireside

each night
a match to paper
and then
the *dance-dance-dancing*
of the blaze
coming alive

the first crackling shot
fired from a twig

ignited
by his hand

a swaying opera
that holds his gaze
each time
as if it was brand new

and inside himself
he rises
to sing
within the roar
of the air-drawing grate

the open flue

until
a minute gone
his eyes
have closed
on the world
and the cares
of a lumpen man

three flames

yellow
within the blue

a constant stream
rising
until it spreads its tongue
to kiss the baffle

    shimmer

the small flames intertwine

    shimmer

the yellow
is inside the blue

   ~

    (puff)

a fire-ball billows

    (puff)

    (puff)

a balloon afloat
that holds its shape
until cooler air

then gone

    (puff)

it is gone

(puff)

the balloon of gas
and fire
is puffed

(puff)

then it is gone

~

the coals
are alive
within the heart

red within black

they release
into the super-hot air
a lick
of yellow

that catches the eye
as it rises

heated from the core
bright

near white

bright

near alive

hot coal hot coal
radiant
within the heart
of fire

high higher bright

burn high
climb higher
burn bright

in contemplation
the fluid movements
mesmerised
her meditation

burn high

the flame
sang its advice

climb higher

a rhythmic pulse
of heat
and distorted brilliance

burn bright

in her dream
she strode

a giant

fire-po

I spoke
into the inferno

I spoke the words soft
lest
I should hear them
aloud

a shiver
and a rising plume
responded
in a swirl

illustrated poetry

>   *a murmur*
>   *a shape*
>   *a glimmer*
>
>   *constant motion*
>   *supple forms*

drawn out of a flow
into soft words
softly spoken

I
move in a suggestive way

I shiver and shape
turning my face
to the warm
where the inferno
speaks its quiet words
to me

I don't hear them clear
but I know the crackle
and the sound
of fire poetry

of two

where

where o flame
do you reach for . . .

strive

where do you aim
and
what do you seek
with your pulsing

do you climb
just as high as ever
until you reach the top

o flame
I sway with you

I reach up

I fall

I reach again
to my height . . .

to beyond to the sky

let us meld
in your heat
we two
burned . . .

molten into
a flowing reaching
wavering determined
wave of fire

of one

we two

returned to the sun

a shimmer
runs over the log

consumes the bark

chars the wood

remembers
what once stood tall

> *leaf and branch*
>
> *the sky*
>
> *the air*
>
> *bird on bough*
>
> *bud burst*

memories given up
with a crackle
and
a sigh

to rise one last time

reminiscent
of the wind

eaten
by the fire

returned —
still hot —
to the sun

drawn to warm

she drew a red bud
on paper

endowed a graceful shape

mesmerizing
as it

> *swayed*
> *and swirled*
> *and rose*

she touched it
with the colours

> *gold*
> *yellow red*
>
> *tangerine*
>
> *a lick of*
> *blue embracing*

she thought the fuel
to make it bright . . .

imagined
shadows

a spark

and drew
her rose
alive

colored pens
placed to one side
and reflections
rebounding all around her

she held her hands
towards her art

rubbed them
to get warm

quickly: a taper

the world
goes quickly by

a switch
has replaced the candle

and the light of suns
in LED
reveals . . .

almost everything

even neon
has come and gone

merely a gas once more

while I . . .

write tapers
against the night

to pulse
as my mind
also
pulses

and cast a soft clarity
where harshness
lies hidden
still

rushlights
to flutter the dark
like a life lived
just outside the fragile light

I am
a slow one
as the world
goes quickly by

the *fast*
that I am too slow
to see

urgency is
a nervousness
that plays
just beneath my skin

I turn away

I turn
away

to
a quiet light

a quiet life

match
to tallow string
I set shadows free

watch them flow

selection

in her sleep
she struck a light

then lit
the beeswax
in its sconce

in the quiet night
she wandered the hall

every room enlivened —
briefly —
into movement
and colour

psychodrama enacted
as the chiaroscuro
touched . . .

transformed

> *here*
> *a flight*
> *astride the eagle*
>
> *next*
> *the desert*
> *and the sky*
>
> *there*
> *the sound of metal struck*
> *by a shovel*
> *at the bottom of an excavation*

she walked on by
inspecting scenarios

scenarios

more scenarios

she walked on by

ready
at any time
to be halted

ready any time
to receive the call
of the right
tonight
scenario

one night in front of the fire

the coal throbs red
the wood is gone

charcoal teeth
are red-smiling

a plume becomes
the blue singer
of three tunes

> *the luff*
> *the flare*
> *the burning*

dragon throat
a promised burn
blackened red
fire purring

and I —
fool me —
creep close
in-drawn
to feel the blaze

we cleaving

what help for me
who looked
into its eye

no help at all

I am
too fallen

light and lies

the candle's light
wavered
when she spoke a lie

something to do
with the tension
of releasing breath

she didn't like that
oh no

she rid herself
of candles

relied instead
on electricity

the power fluctuated
when she spoke a lie

something to do
with static
when she found herself
tense

she didn't like that
oh no

she did all her work —
her business —
in the sunlight hours

did you hear about
the sunspot
activity . . .

she didn't like that
no no
she did not like that
at all

a philosophy of fragile times

when he turned the hourglass
the sand ran
up
as he knew it would

deep contemplation
so often turns life
on its head

a lamp's flame
only rises
while the candlewick
burns down

in the end
there is a residue
of blackened ash
in a wax pool

melted into a softness
that *was*
for a little while

meanwhile
the level of the sand
is rising

some kind of time
is running up

running out

lapsing

some kind of life
is over

with a flutter
like a puff of soft breath
the sound of the sand
departs

the glass is full
and the darkness
clings
to a shape
that

      once upon
      an hourglass

held
a lamp's light

chiaroscuro thinking

he thought in thoughts
of light and shade

his dappled mood
thought with them

> *smile to frown*
> *to absence*
> *of mind*

he thought
some bright

some duller

so much
duller

at night
he closed his eyes
to dream
and the dark
was pricked with colour

his dreams
pursued the trail
of his thoughts
from light
to shade

first the one
and then . . .

around
and around

carnevale

dressed
as epiphany
she juggled colours
in the air

across . . .

between . . .

under and over . . .

they wove —
like ribbons —
into figures of eight
and
into bows

and once
into *her* name

a fuse alight

they each descended

to be caught . . .
and then thrown aloft

up
into the air
again

forming a layering
of colour

then
she swallowed one

the rest
still in the air

up

she swallowed one

the rest . . .

one
at a time

until
the darkness of sleep
swallowed *her*
in turn
and her entire
carnevale

aspiring to white

where he walked
he left the footprints . . .

the *spoor*
of a better man

every step
held within itself
a small idea
of *more*

behind him —
as time passed —
each imprint
slowly disappeared

behind him
the *might have been*
dispersed
day by day
and wind by wind
until
the last dust
was gone
and hard clay
all that remained

he bent low
to strike a match

to
ignite his paper

yellow flared
an idea
of something . . .

more

an aspiration
to rise up

burn hot

and to transform
a yellow *self*
into white

one flame

she focused her mind
on the weaving motion
of flames
in the firebox

tremors
not quite rhythmic
in their pulsation

closer . . .

she concentrated
on the gyration
of *one*

    striving for height

    running
    a small rill
    on its own tinder

    bobbing down
    to almost disappear

    striving again
    to reach up

she found
she could narrow
her awareness

shut out
all other flames
that burnt —
so earnestly —
their own faggots of wood

to watch
and be
with just the one
gyring shape

thought to herself

  I
 am alone

two times

he tried to achieve
the union
of two
separates . . .

two *individuals*

with his match
he lit a pair of candles

then
when both
were alive —
bobbing softly
in a gentle draught —
he brought them together

each
bent inwards
to meet the other

> *brought close enough*
> *to embrace*
> *and then*
> *unite*
>
> *two*
> *into one*

but . . .

no

from that body
of small fire
rose two heads

two mountain tops

weaving
as they burned

two
could come *so close*
but
the pair
would not be merged

no no
it was always meant to be
two
times one

pivot

I am of
the ascending gyre

the fire
rises
from within me

when I skip away —
so lithely —
to the left
the blaze skips
also

rightwards

yellow
sits above my blue
red —
the *vibrance* —
my heart
beneath

I am the pivot
for this fire

and she
matches me

my every move

illumination

a pinpoint shone —
a bright little spark —
when he picked up his pen
to write

> *a poet*
> *a lyricist*
>
> *a dreamer*

and it shone —
a little brighter —
when the first words
kissed the page

their imprint
a line
of ignition
etched across the white

and it burned
radiant and truer
with every illuminating word

room soft lit

> *fire dancing*

words

> *such wondrous words*

then dimmed —
drawn away
out of the air —
as he penned nearer
to the end

finally . . .

no sound at all
of pen
scratching upon paper

the darkness —
black
and uniform —
lay everywhere
that he could see

a thousand (cackling)

in the hearth
my fire
is a thousand eyes
gazing out
through the glass

in my hearth
the fire speaks
in the voices
of a thousand tongues

in my hearth
devils dance
they have burned away
all their clothing

> *it is a pagan story*
>
> *a pagan joy*
>
> *a revelry*

I watched them
from my place
on this side
of the glass

I watched them
twist
contort
and twirl

I watched them
staring . . .

hypnotised

> *the flick*
> *and flare*
> *the flagration*

and
I watched them
drawn in —
nearer —
to their lewd display

I watched
and I watched
until . . .

a cackle

and I heard them
laugh

in the black cell

the doors
the walls
the floor

the spaces
that are corridors
of black . . .

of darkness

footsteps
pace
up and down

up
and down

unseen
but casting
an echo

a *solid* sound . . .

is the heavy tread
of boot
on floor

the door into the cell
holds a window

> *cool to the touch*
> *darkened glass*

no light can travel
in or out

no illumination
disturbs the corridor

the footsteps —
the treading boots —
stop

dull eyes
peer in
through the smoky lens

to gaze
hungry
on the shivers
of a captive

slowly contorting . . .

      twisting
      weaving whispering
      attempting . . .

somehow
to hold the shadows
at bay

wax
weeps tearful rivulets
that cannot be seen
from the corridor side
of the window

a small
cold white
is all

the heavy tread
steps away again

ponderous
with the carriage
of dead
dark
weight

reading to a familiar soft gleam

by the gleam
of the eyes
of her cat
she read the news

> *a complete infestation of rats*
> *down town*
>
> *the hazards*
> *of climbing trees*
>
> *some old mog*
> *called* eight
> *used to be known*
> *as* seven

the cat
blinked

she turned a page

> *sixteen games to play*
> *for mouse*
> *and*
> *for mouser*
>
> *hackles raised –*
> *a static storm*
>
> *close encounters*
> *with a feral*
>
> *litter fine*
> *(seven kits)*

the cat
looked up
into her eyes
as he shied away

a soft gleam
and
a familiar
that still revealed . . .

too much

about solitude

where do you go
to find
your solitude

he thought about

his house

the clutter
of his rooms

the gentle and the fierce
demands
of belonging to a home
and
to a family

he thought about

his garden

always in a state
of change
from the first sprouts
of springtime
to the autumn decays . . .

winter sleeping

he thought about

the sky above

the vast expanse of it

of cloud
of blue
of sun and moon

day time and night time

he thought about

a prison cell

enclosure
within walls
in both
light and dark

with nothing else
but mind

turning over thoughts
and dreams

rehearsing
how to write them

he thought about

a weaving flame
wavering
like water running
up
a burning log

yellow blue
and swirl

and twirl

in answer
to a question asked . . .

he *thinks*
it was a question
asked

coming to you (moth song)

I desire
to beat my wings
in the pool
of your light

I would love to rise —
much higher —
in your warming air

> *ha*
> *ha*

you will burn me
I know it

> *ha*
> *ha*
> *ha*

I will burn

I am flying
around
your glamour

you tempt me . . .

I tempt you

I love you
so

I am approaching
your embrace

here I am

I am coming . . .

to you

around, my love

around
and around

despite myself
I return
one more time

I go

around
and around

I know . . .

I *think* I know
what it means
to burn

go around

and I try *so* hard
to keep
a little distance

and around

but that *heat* . . .

it makes me feel
this
is what
I'm looking for

around around

around I go again

closer . . .

A Cleansing Flame

I move away

always
a little closer

and around

ah well
if it is my fate

if I must crash
and burn away
well
so I will

and
so I will

go around

I come
a little closer

who can —
in the very end of ends —
who can
resist his death

resist
his calling in life

one time

one last time
around

around you
my love

finding seclusion

she read the account —
written by another —
of a search
for solitude

how a visit
to isolation

    a seclusion within a room

was insufficient

how companionship

    friends
    small crowds

engendered loneliness

and how —
in the end —
only gazing into
the kindled pyre
could achieve
what she was seeking

    the sense
    of a positive solitariness
    without any feeling
    of loss

she read the account
again

at the conclusion found herself
content

slow world

the world
is
a difficult book
to comprehend

a harsh reading
makes each word
twist
and leap
between colours

meanings change
inconstant
at each new visitation

> *turn the power off*
>
> *put a match*
> *to the spill*
>
> *light the taper*
>
> *soft the light*
>
> *slow it*
> *right down*

words
can find
their definitions . . .

their *intentions*

the world is
once again
merely the place in which
I live

another page
will bring tomorrow

and
if I look
into the heart
of the burning candle
I *know*

soon
I
will begin to dream

striving for a ride

should I dream
that the spark
rises higher
as it strives

should I dream
that it carried me
up . . .

until
we both rose
beyond the heavens
on a draught

the spark and I . . .

I . . .

I

should I dream
that it took me

up and away . . .

up
with me riding

up
the spark seeking higher

and me

in *that* dream
I would ride

beyond smoke

a small tongue
twisted . . .

ran
up and down a twig
as it burned

before finally —
bobbing and wavering
at the end of the wood —

it burned
with a desire
to climb above —
beyond —
and it leapt up . . .

and it leapt up

as it could
to follow
the shimmering air

at last
in its dismay
it strove mightily . . .

CRACK!

it drew in the air . . .

CRACK!

and died down
again

as with a

CRACK!

all its energy expired

it was small
again

.

.

.

a single spark
rose

gleaming

swirling
as it climbed the warm air

higher
and further
beyond the birthing fire

beyond smoke

angels dance

how many dance
on a point

that bobs
and weaves
with each breath released

as it reaches —
strives —
for more

how many
as the battle
between day
and dark
is fought
in empty spaces

between the wax
and the string
and
the rising bud

curved
to sway so
and
to rise

angels bathe
in burning light

count them

count them
in their shadows
cast
as negative impressions
on the wall

flickered away

their essence
in its ascent
wavers

wavers
into smoke
then
is gone

to clear the smoke

she had blackened
the glass

the cotton wicking
had not been straight

and the lamp
now
is not the same
as it had been
the night before
when
a match
had made a flare
and
the flare
had become a beacon

the feeling
of *warm*
had pervaded

now . . .

there is smoke
in the lantern

the beacon has become
a frail thing
and the future
too hard
to glimpse

she wishes —
just *one* wish —
that she had taken
a little more time

time enough
for smoke to clear
so she could see

solitary intrusion

my light
is solitary

only I
may carry it

yours
should not shine
where *I* can see it

how can I
be solitary

      alone alone alone

how can I
when you shine
where I must be

you are vexatious
to me

you seek
your solitude
right there
yet you shine
so close
to me
that
I must see
you

go
away

     go go go

go away
with your light
where I won't see

go away
and be solitary
go

leave *me*
to myself

return (of the season)

the cold of the day
marked the first
real
turning of the year

autumn
had come
in buffets of bluster
and a swaying
of trees

the chill
set him to wood
then
to paper

to kindling

the first fire
of the season
sent up a secret of smoke
to explore
all means of escape

and he swam
through the air
within it
even as he closed off
every avenue
and path

the first flame
the first smoke
the first
reverie

the year had —
at last —
turned

a plate (to row)

ah . . .
seeing

he made a sound
a dismissive
snort

anyone
can see

look

I put a thing –
call it a plate –
in front of you

you see it
alright

you know it
can name it

it is there
and you
comprehend it

that is seeing

imagining
though

ahhhh

there
is a different thing!

the object you saw
I imagine
as something else

your plate
is my
boat

I can
visualise
rowing it
across an ocean
of tea

that
is what I
can hold as a picture
in my mind

while you
gaze
at your paltry plate

practicing prudence

oh no
sir

she said

I would never
risk
all of my light

no

even
when I'm dreaming —

yes
even then —
I keep my shutters
closed in

only enough
to see
a little way
in front of me

that
is my rule
sir

gospel of a flame

you may sleep
before the fire

nodding . . .

there you go

you may sleep
before the blazing log

nodding . . .

yes
there you go

but you cannot sleep
to a candle's slow flutter

it will sway
to keep you
awake

you cannot sleep
before a candle
moving on the wall
in its shadow shape

sleep
with the fire

sleep before the blaze
but
stay awake
to watch the candle
rouse you
from your stupor

alone (together)

the flame
is alone
but for me

I watch it
flutter
at the faintness
of my breath

I
am alone
but for its gleam

watch me
flicker
to the pulse
of mellow light

we are seperate
          (*flutter*)
breathing
in our own ways

feeling
          (*flutter*)
the play of air

watching
          (*flutter*)
the play
that is a small life

together

a longing (to flutter)

and does
the fire

    beyond the glass
    above the oil
    atop the braided cotton

ever long
for freedom

it burns
as it must burn
yielding light
and climbing
within its confines

does it never
wonder
with naked desire

how it might feel
to flutter
in the caresses
the tender touch
of a gentle
untrammeled breeze

oh
to waver

to make
shadows

oh
to burn high
like riding
on air

and to move
as only fire can move

> *ta-ta*
> *ta*
> *ta-ta-ta*

I wonder
does *that* flame
there
ever wish
for the flutter

the moment of daring
that would skate
the edge of extinction

the fire

> *behind the glass*
> *above the oil*
> *atop the braided cotton*

burns bright

and
it burns steady

in the lantern heart

in the heart
of the lantern . . .

there
I will place
a memory

warm and bright

a
recollection

in the place
in the heart
where such colours live
I will substitute
something that I knew
once

radiant

a small
heart keepsake

you know
as I know
all the things we did

I recall them
so well
but I have seen
those sweet memories
fading
until only I
can find them

so I will place
in the lantern heart
a memory
for safer keeping

another —
a soft
warm recollection —
and another

to burn bright
enough
that you and I
can find them

always

reverie (gone)

I live inside
a reverie

a candle moved
by its own
current

in the warm
of it
I reside

overtaken

by reverie

by my own
heat

I shine brightly

and then
I am gone

and
then

I
am gone

time well

how long
can you flicker

how fast
is your burn

contorting in shadows
time goes

time goes

I contort
in the shadows

~

how heavy
is a grain of sand

what do you do
when your well
is a hollow

time falls
away

time
falls away

my well
is always deeper
when time falls
away

crude: the marvel

he was crude
stuff

he was raw

but
when he lit himself . . .

oh

a flare
of bright white light

he burned

until —
clean again —
he *shone*

he *warmed*

he was
a marvel

The Psychoanalysis of Fire

seeing within

when she looked
at herself

cast her mind
inward

she could not see
the truth
anymore

the truth
was painted
in the silver
of the mirror
but . . .

what she saw
when she looked
inside herself
was only . . .

what she
believed

why no warning

they are the same

he thought
while rubbing his finger
ruefully

the sting of pain
left behind
from the stab
of a pin

and
the sensation of burning
that lingered
on his thumb
from when he held the lit match
a little
too long

they are nearly
the same

why
was I never warned
by my father
of the danger
in pins

the one use

there is only
one
good
use

for a fire . . .

he spoke
as he turned to face
away
from the heat

warming his behind
against the chilly night

. . . only the one use . . .

moving
finally

reluctantly

to resume
his chair

. . . and that . . .

as he fixed his gaze
on the grate

filled to overflowing
by the radiance
of hot coals
and embers

. . . is
to look

at it . . .

he forced an uprising
frenzy
of sparks
with a vicious stab
of the poker

    . . . to look at it
    and

    to think

not ash

I am here
in the rouge

my faces
show red

dappling
with the night
as the dance
flows on

I will feed here
I will
grow

I will whisper
in underneath tones

I will roar
and you
will know
god

for a moment

my moment

I will fade
a little . . .

only a little

I will sing
my tiny blues

and I will
small myself
to distort
a little breath
of air

still rising
in the morning
when life
is gone

the morning
of grey
and white . . .

a suggestion
only

a suggestion
warm
of the fire
that I was

the abandonment
of *burned*

of embers
still alive

remember me
in colours
red

not
in shades
of ash

guardian of the flame

if I

were the one
who came
to steal
your fire

would you
hide yourself

hide
the heat
from me

or
would you
take my hand

place it
near the flame

on the flame

in the flame

to be
the flame

if *I*
were the one

would you hide
the fire

the alchemist's fire

masculine principles
strike
at the centre

feminine principles
veiled
from without

he muttered to himself
as he mixed
his compound

bedraggled
through his own neglect

filled
with hunger

yet unaware
of being
hungry

of the last time
he had eaten

masculine . . .

center . . .

feminine . . .

with the last
mutter

the last
ingredient

the last mixing

pounding

stirring

he applied
a match

and
as the material
reacted . . .

the compound
quickened

a sinuous plume of

grey

white

blue

smoke

rose
languorously

twisting
around itself

seeming to . . .

pause

for a moment

before twirling away
higher

then
dissipating

he stood still

silent

gazing
at what had been

felt himself
in *awe*

perhaps
in *life*

before the crackling sound
rising from the beaker
reminded him
of work
still to be done

for the first time
in days
he felt . . .

ravenous

yes

soon
he must eat

fizz

in my body
is
a fire

> *pulsing*
>
> *a breath*
> *within the blood*
>
> *fizz and crackle*

I am contained
but
inside myself
I burn

I watch you
in the night

I see the way
you shine

I would light you
brighter still

> *fizz and crackle*
>
> *inside myself*
> *I burn*

I sometimes wonder
if we should meet

my orbit
casual
in your path

would we separate
with mere words
or

    fizz and crackle

would we burn

electricity
demands its movement
positive

you and I
the stellar floor

    fizz and crackle

    fizz and crackle

do we
not
burn

what it is (I call it)

what
is the flame
before
it is lit

is it
still
the flame

is it heat
at all

is it
cold

chill

gone

an absence
that is simply
not

what
is a matchstick
then

is it a spark
engaged
in a long wait

in seeking
perhaps

is it a predator
hiding
until . . .

a moment
of becoming

until it
is

I call that
a match

I call it
genesis

the physics of the unconscious

lead
is in the air

no one
is shooting bullets
but . . .

what *can* rise
must rise

fire
eats air
like a starving child

grows
to fill a new suit

every
new suit

I swim
just a little bit
above
the water

admire
the trickle
and the flow

but
personally I prefer
not to get
my feet wet

floating on my back
my dream

my dream
is
gravity

the entertainer (last show)

she smiled —
showed teeth —
as she performed

first
juggling

small batons

    two

    three

    four

lit
and thrown . . .

and caught

over and again

a fiery pinwheel
returned
by hand
to the air

returned —
via parabola —
to hand

then
the longer pole

alight
at both ends

    swaying

    leaping

she
and her fires
in accord

mesmerizing the night
with the fluidity
of their movements

the growl
as they whirled

finally
swallowing

the volcano
into
her mouth

a fireball
puffed
blown
back into the air

again

again

and lastly
truly
lastly

she burned

Fragments from A Poetics of Fire

bird of fire

phoenix
am I

somehow
I stand before you

you know
I know
this
is an impossible
truth

I have died
yet
here I am
alive

reborn

renewed

or maybe . . .

maybe
I am only
resurrected

who can tell

not I

this air
tastes
of sweet things

phoenix I am
consumed
in my own fire

tongues
of red and gold and life
licked me
black
to the bone

to death

to the voice
that spoke
into my name

     I see you

while the conflagration
cleansed my soul
the voice held
a taste of *me*
in its timbre

     I see you

     yes

     I see you

     alive

imagine no history

it was the work
of an instant

no more

imagination
has no history

imagination is
a thing

a time

a place

someone
who *wasn't* there

is
now here

I saw it
so it
is

must
be

medium

she thought
deeply

examined

familiarised

she was a writer
a poet

and she thought
deeply
before taking up
her pen

she knew
what she wished to write
for
a clear idea
had formed
within her mind

and it was this
this thought
that needed to be
expressed

documented

as her pen
touched
onto the paper
the words began

flowed out
like water
in a stream

all her thinking
ceased

now
there was only
the image
writing itself
upon the page

furiously

frenetically

the ephemeral
assuming

becoming
something like
a corporeal form

until . . .

it stopped

it was complete

she put the pen
down

as always
she felt a little
amazed
a little stunned

for what was written
was not
her thought

although

yes

in a way
it was

what was written
was . . .

an *idea*
that had chosen
to express itself
through the medium
that she was

rake the coals

he finds
a ruby

stone still inflamed

clear the ash
yesterday

let the air touch
today

let the spark be
tomorrow

pink wood
from a mountain forest

red wood
from the flood plains

yellow wood that fell
by the way

rake the coals
find the fire opal

the precious stones
hidden in ash

kiss them
each
with a breath of air

give us life
for another day

first touch

she waited
for the sun to rise

standing
faced to the east

unmoving

she watched
for the shape of morning

a slow encroachment
across the hills

hueing the black
into a more pallid shade

a grey

the gold of the clouds
was the sun
surely
rising

she reached . . .

she passed
the point where
she could see her hands

held still before her
facing
in the direction of the sun

watching
waiting
the advance of day

the shadow
that was night
retreated
to take solace
behind her

and as the sun's first ray
touched
an outstretched finger
she burned

inferno
to
ash

she burned

bird alight

I saw the bird
rise
into the blue

leaned back
to watch it fly

saw it consumed

.

.

.

broken things

broken things will fall
as though flung
away from the heart
before performing an arc

the far half
of a parabola

like the weightless ash
that rises
from a backyard bonfire

like feathers
suddenly independent
dancing with the help
of a surreptitious breeze

a seeming of ichor

a thunder roll
of sound

smoke . . .

but I could not read
its message

bird alight

bird aflame

bird burning
in the blue

then
in small drifts
to the ground

and smoke and smoulder

he came
searching
for a drink

not really so very much
to seek

cola
lemonade

orange juice

even water
in a glass
if it came to it

any store
on the street
could surely
have obliged him

but
one by one —
slightly ahead of him
as he walked —
they each shut their doors

drew the shutters

his thirst
remained unquenched
while he slowly flamed
a path
down main street

something about him
made good people
hesitate
and the heat he raised
did not assist the impression
they formed of him

it is hard to help
a man
so much on fire without you
yourself
becoming burned

as he walked —
in a kind of stagger —
smouldering footprints
continued to burn around the edges
showing the way
he had approached
the town

three curious boys
gathered around one of them
to conduct an examination

poking it
with a stick
though they remained
well behind the man
and his —
hotter —
more recent steps

it was a small child
in the end —
a young girl —
who ran out
ahead of him
to place a glass
of water into his path

and while the town
watched
he paused

leaned over
to pick up the glass

to drink
the clear
cool *vitae*
of fresh water

he bent towards it
and collapsed
into grey ash

and smoke
and smoulder

among us

he wore his hat
brim low
to keep his face
withdrawn

hidden
under a shadow

didn't say much
in a voice
that sounded cracked
and dry

more a shape
than a man

drawing dark around him
like a cloak
filled
with nothing

no
he didn't say much
but if you ever glimpsed
his eyes

you'd see a fire
just waiting to burn

and you'd need to
look away
quick
because *he*
is a fire

getting ready
to burn

a small essence (and an unusual phenomenon)

everyone who saw
agreed
as she did herself

it was an
unusual
phenomenon

she had looked
to the sun
to watch rays
dancing

had swum
in the waters
of a shimmer
in the desert

but
this time
when she cut herself
she bled

small droplets
of red flame
that seemed —
almost —
to splash and spread
when they touched the ground

she could only watch
along with the rest
amazed
as a small part . . .

a small essence
of *herself*
incinerated

it is (was)

it is a fire

it is a man

I blink . . .

it is the smoke
of a thing
that *was*

I blink . . .

it *is*

a feather for his hat

he could see the bird
from a distance

black and raucous
it flew
toward him

with every other wing-flap
it uttered a harsh call
and vomited

    spat

a bolus of heated ire
like lightning
when it strikes

behind the bird
a pocked trail
of small fires
burned

before it
he waited

he was not some kind
of hero
but he understood
that this
was an appointed task

and so he waited
while the bird
flapped
and crowed
and spat

low it came
making no attempt
at deviation

while —
stilled —
he stood

tense
and waiting

when it happened
it was over
quickly

one moment
the bird was ejecting
its vitriolic gout

the next . . .

he had reached out
up
and caught it

hugged it fiercely to himself
heat and spit and call
until . . .

it was *himself*
that he was hugging

there was no *bird*
that was not
a part of *him*

as he called
a wild
raucous cry
the last traces of bird fire
burning along the now obsolete
back path
gave way

died out

he bent to the ground
to gently lift
one black flight feather
which he fixed
somberly
into the band
of his hat

feather to fly

last consumed
the last
remained

both covering and revealing
the modest mound
of ash
gradually being eaten away
by its own small coterie
of flames

almost
as a final act

as
a conclusion
to combustion

a single black feather
rose
in the near elegance
of a plume
of blue smoke

released
by the band
of the hat
to fly

he dreams the spoken tongue

when the wind
speaks
with tongues that burn

I will fly
like a bird
of perdition

close my eyes
feel myself
rising

lifted

when the wind
is lit

the bird will fly

dance

way-way

what is the song
of fire

way-way-way

what is that music

tremors shiver
up and down
and wavering

what time will keep
the rhythm
in the soul

way-way

way-way

way-way-way
way-oh-way-oh

kiss kiss
the heat arising

way-oh-way

the fire dance

now the remembrance of fire

as a child
it had been apparent
that he enjoyed play
with matches

paper

small twigs

at first
there had been concern
but
no spark ever seemed
to escape him

always
they were extinguished
as though
they had never been

while *he*
seemed . . .

brighter

happier
after he had lit
and burned

only now
so many years later
did the long tongues
wag

now
everything seemed so clear
so interconnected

dream of empty

in restless sleep —
as she dreamed —
it rose
and swirled

the devourer
unleashed to colour the skies
red

a storm
wild and unbridled
burning
where it struck

grey ash
in its wake

cinders and char

in restless sleep
she dreamed it flew
in black

and knew
an empty place
within

a dream of completion

he felt himself
a little mad

    possessed

    dreaming destruction

    longing for a greater
    completeness

to his own ears
even his laughter
was the cackling
of a conflagration

always
when he closed his eyes
he saw the working
of the fire
rising

felt the heat
of it within

he knew
that at times
he smouldered

start again prometheus

every day
I begin again

every day
from nothing

so
when I stand
it is my own design

I rise
to the morning

from naught

I think
myself

      again

into the morning

flay me (jealously)

I live
in the borderland

I am not a man
I am not
a god

perhaps I am
both these things
in a fusion

in my hand
I hold a living light

mine to keep
or mine
to give

in my mind
I hold
an inferno

I know where it resides

it is mine
to burn
as I please

so
flay me
for thievery

      I hold the fire

flay me
for impudence

      I hold the fire

one day
I will fly

so flay me
jealously

for I hold
your fire

become breath

the fire
is a transformation

cleansed
to a state
of purity

devoured
to a state
of ash

blown away
in a state
by the wind

rapture

rapture in the motion

rapture
in the sway

rapture rising
reaching to the blue
of the sky

rapture in the ember
rapture
in the pulse

rapture in
containment
of the heart
lying quiet

so begin

begin

add a stick
of *rapture-waiting*
to burn

begin

at stars

each night
I roar up at stars

I shake my mane
at injustice

it is not right
that I am
here

I am the sun
I am
majesty
but
I am aground
so
hear me
roar

ROAR

loud enough
they will hear it

ROAR

and

ROAR

some day
they *must* hear it

ROAR and ROAR

I will make them
sorrow

rue

rue and regret

each night
I watch
and then
I roar
up

up

I *ROAR*
at the stars

hail the poet king

we-ell in this world
the poet
is king

we-e-ell
in this world
the poet
is *the* king

he sings to you
in images

lets you see
to the other
side

gives you solace
here
when life
is hard

the poet is king

the poet
is *the* king

all hail
his verse

all hail his rhyme

his stories paint
pictures

his pictures
raise
the veil

he lets you find
solace

when your peace
has gone
to hell

we-ell
we-e-e-ell
all hail
the poet king
of this world
that you
are living in

poet (demised)

there he is
a poet boy
wandering

his mind
on fire

every where he looks
he sees
the possibility
of stanza

every still life
becomes
an image
that he *should* turn
into verse

he hardly has
the wit
anymore
to feed himself

believes
that he takes nourishment
from imagining a thought
becoming *real*

so *real*
that anyone who reads it
will believe it

will believe *him*

the act
of writing down
is a creation that first
becomes
and then
runs

there is no stopping it

he does not want to

something like
creation
lives in the ink
that he pushes out
from his pen

something like
creator
as he dreams it

there he is
the *no-hope* boy

clever
yeah
but he's not
smart

not smart enough
to survive

he will write his own
coffin
will write down
his own shallow grave

one day
he'll write
his demise

his own shallow
demise

the poet boy

impossible

but
how can I believe
in cinders

how
can I believe
the blaze

neither one
is the source
of it

neither has the germ
to *be*

yet
here I am

every feather of me
still a-smoulder

two times
I have burned

in the death
that folded
upon itself

and in
the rejuvenation

that explosion
of myself

close your eyes
I am not much
now
to see

and
as I stand here
I find that
I must believe

in a thing
I know
is impossible

brightly

do you burn
when you gaze
at the sun

when you burn
do you become
a fireball

circling terra
firma

do you burn
just to die

.

.

.

look on the sun
once again

live

live on
brightly

time (and temperature)

time stops

I beat my wings

my temperature
just half
a flame

from fire

if (the fire)

if I were
the fire

how much of me
would burn

would I be
resistant
to myself

would it be
just like water
when I bend my head
low
into the flame

do you think
the street
would be safe
from me
if I needed
to buy my bread

or would I burn away
reduced
to ash

nothing
but a tendril

a rising twirl
of smoulder

if I
were the fire
what would happen
to me

to you

away (I burn)

I beat my wings
upon the nest

I burn
before I fly

    away

    away

I am a fire
in the sky

    away

I burn up
so high

burn song

the song
is a torch

hear me sing

burn my ears

raise me
on a vector

soaring

searing

raise me
on a vector

the song
is a plume
is a flare
is a torch
is
the fire

singing

singing
I burn

flown

I saw the flash
of a phoenix bird
as I sat
quite still
beside the fire

red
in the tree
as the smoke
rose twirling
above

just a bird

I thought

only a bird

but
what a time
to come and call

what a time
to visit

when the smoke
shows a shape
and the bird holds
all
of the colour

and while my gaze
roves all over —
searching —
a sound
draws my eye
to the fire

one coal —
red —
has fallen

a cloud of sparks
from the first . . .

from
another

I look again

the bird above
is gone

only smoke
remains

a shape
left rising

while another coal
flowers its orange-red —
kissed by a breeze —
and then it too
falls

no spark
this time
the bird has flown

in surrender

the crystal
enchants
the wandering
of a dreaming eye

something
in the movement
calls attention

and
in the middle of a dream
within
the undulations
of a vision
it becomes flamenco
in a red skirt

with a flare
while the castanets
crackle

I pause
in my aimless drift

taken
by this vision

it is illusion
I know

a hallucination
of half-sleep

but I am running
in a pair
within the roar

twirling

un-burning

held
rapt and safe
in the warm arms
of a trance

I hear
the chorus sing
basso

they are a roaring
of demons

raising voices
that start
away . . .

away below

they surround me
and I
embrace them

dancing
I
have surrendered

a cleansing flame

rendered
to a taper

arm
upraised

he ignited
his impurities

those that were
himself
and that stood
so rigidly
as *him*

then —
slowly —
he burned

> *his unclean self*

> *his*
> *incompleteness*
> *and deficits*

burned

> *a flame is yellow*
> *a flame is blue*
> *a flame*
> *is white*

and so he burned
until the radiance —
so warm in its honesty —
faded
to grey

to dark

until
a muddling pool
of tallowed *stuff*
and
a dispersing black
of smoke
were *all*

he was gone
but
the shape of him —
burned clean away —
the shape that *once*
he was
stood clear
stood pure

clean

Bachelard Source Materials

Gaston Bachelard, French Philosopher lived from 27 June 1884 to 16 October 1962. The series of poems and poetry in this book has drawn inspiration from the following publications by Bachelard, translated into English.

Intuition of the Instant by Gaston Bachelard (1932) Eileen Rizo-Patron (Translator) Northwestern University Press, 2013

The New Scientific Spirit, by Gaston Bachelard (1934), A. Goldhammer (Translator) Beacon Pr; 1st Edition (1984)

The Psychoanalysis of Fire, by Gaston Bachelard (1938), A.C. Ross (Translator) (1964).

Lautréamont, Gaston Bachelard (1939), Robert S. Dupree (Author), James Hillman (Author), Dallas Institute Publications; Reprint Edition (2012)

Water and Dreams: An Essay on the Imagination of Matter by Gaston Bachelard (1942), Edith R. Farrell (Translator) (1983.

Air and Dreams: An Essay on the Imagination of Movement, by Gaston Bachelard (1943), Edith R. Farrell (Translator), Frederick Farrell (Translator) Dallas Institute Publication Dallas Institute Publications (1988)

Earth and Reveries of Will: An Essay on the Imagination of Matter by Gaston Bachelard (1943), Kenneth Haltman (Translator) Dallas Institute Publications (2002)

Earth and Reveries of Repose: An Essay on Images of Interiority by Gaston Bachelard (1948), Mary McAllester Jones (Translation), Dallas Institute Publications (2011)

Dialectic of Duration. Gaston Bachelard (1950), Mary McAllester Jones (Translator), Rowman & Littlefield Publishers; (2016)

The Poetics of Space by Gaston Bachelard (1958), Maria Jolas (Translator) Penguin Classics (1964).

The Poetics of Reverie, by Gaston Bachelard (1960), Daniel Russell (Translator) Beacon Press; New Ed Edition (1971)

The Flame of a Candle, by Gaston Bachelard, (1961), Joni Caldwell (Translator) Dallas Institute Publications (1988).

The Right to Dream by Gaston Bachelard (1970), J.A. Underwood

(Translator) Dallas Institute Publications (1988)
Fragments of a Poetics of Fire, by Gaston Bachelard, Kenneth Haltman (Translator), Dallas Institute Publications (1988)
On Poetic Imagination and Reverie, by Gaston Bachelard, Colette Gaudin (Translator) Spring Publications; (2014)

Author Information

Frank Prem has been a storytelling poet since his teenage years. He has been a psychiatric nurse through all of his professional career, which now exceeds forty years.

He has been published in magazines, online zines, and anthologies in Australia, and in a number of other countries, and has both performed and recorded his work as spoken word.

He lives with his wife in the beautiful township of Beechworth in North East Victoria, Australia.

Connect with Frank

Find Frank at his website www.FrankPrem.com, or through Social Media online at Facebook, X (Twitter), Instagram and YouTube.

Other Published Works

Free Verse Poetry

Small Town Kid (2018)
Devil In The Wind (2019)
The New Asylum (2019)
Herja, Devastation - With Cage Dunn (2019)
Walk Away Silver Heart (2020)
A Kiss for the Worthy (2020)
Rescue and Redemption (2020)
Pebbles to Poems (2020)
The Garden Black (2022)
A Specialist at The Recycled Heart (2022)
Ida: Searching for The Jazz Baby (2023)
From Volyn to Kherson (2023)
Alive Is What You Feel (2023)
White Whale (2024)
Pilgrim Volume 1 - Illustrated by Leanne Murphy (2024)
A Poetry Archive Volume 1 (2024)
A Poetry Archive Volume 2 (2024)
A Poetry Archive Volume 3 (2024)
A Poetry Archive Volume 3 (2024)

Picture Poetry/Spoken Image

Voices (In The Trash) (2020)
The Beechworth Bakery Bears (2021)
Sheep On The Somme (2021)
Waiting For Frank-Bear (2021)
A Lake Sambell Walk (2021)
A Few Places Near Home (2023)
The Cielonaut (2024)

What Readers Say

A Kiss For The Worthy

A Celebration of Life Written in Thoughtful Bursts of Poetic Expression
—C M C (United States)

With every verse, I found myself reflecting about myself, my life, and the world.
—K

Rescue and Redemption

The passion of love in its many forms explored by one for another.
—J L (United States)

I've enjoyed every word, every breath. Every moment within the life of these stories.
—C D (Australia)

Sheep On The Somme

Museums and archivists take note~sell this in your gift shops, preserve it in your archives. Professors, teachers~share with your students.
—A R C (United States)

(This) book is a beautiful and graphic tribute to all those brave men and women who gave their lives for their countries between 1914 and 1918.
—R C (South Africa)

Ida: Searching for The Jazz Baby

I found myself deeply moved by the presentation of Ida's elusive, illusionary life.
—E G (United States)

He gives her a depth and vulnerability that the press didn't.
— A C (United Kingdom

The Garden Black

Prem creates verse that illuminates our world, its experiences and history.

—S C (United Kingdom)

Prem's poetry reminds that life is fragile and fleeting ... both harsh and beautiful.

—D G K (Canada)

A Few Places Near Home

The author has captured many beautiful images in this book, and is a wonderful photographer as well as a poet. This book would make a beautiful coffee table book filled with moving prose to make us ponder with gorgeous accompanying images.

—D K (Canada))

www.FrankPrem.com